ENDORSEMENTS

"Current philosophical assumptions taught in our secular universities are seldom addressed, simply assumed. I witnessed this in my studies at Columbia University. This manual will help you understand major issues with simple well-stated answers. You will want to refer to it again and again. In my humble opinion, every ministerial student should have a copy!"

—L. David Beckman, ThD, President Emeritus, Colorado Christian University, Denver

"*The Road Most Traveled* is concise and stimulating . . . a superb job of communicating philosophical ideas and their consequences in a brief compass. Its vivid portrayal of the dead ends to which popular roads lead should help many to assess the outcomes of their lifestyles."

—Gordon Lewis, PhD, Senior Professor of Theology and Philosophy, Denver Seminary

"I think this is an excellent tool to use on the college campus and elsewhere. Last year one of our student leaders, a philosophy major, and I conducted a weekly discussion with three atheist men. All were churched, intelligent, bright, freshmen honors college students. And all had made conscious decisions to turn from a belief in God to a position of atheism. This booklet would have been a great tool to have them read and then discuss. Yes, it could be well used by campus missionaries."

—Michael C. Dickens, Regional Campus Specialist, Campus Ambassadors, Mission to the Americas

The author is indebted to Vernon Grounds, Chancellor, Denver Seminary, whose PhD thesis was on *The Concept of Love in the Psychology of Sigmund Freud,*
Gordon Lewis, PhD, Senior professor of theology and philosophy, Denver Seminary,
R.S. Beal, Jr., PhD, biological scientist, former Dean of the Graduate School, No. Arizona University, Flagstaff,
Gene R. Marlatt, PhD, former Academic Dean, Colorado Christian University, Denver, and
Janice Boville, instructor of philosophy, Southwestern College and Grand Canyon University, both in Phoenix.

The Road Most Traveled

Solutions to Life's Problems by the Movers and Shapers of Our World – *And the Consequences*

David P. Beal

WINEPRESS WP PUBLISHING

Scripture references marked KJV are taken from the King James Version of the Bible.

Matthew 7:13–14 and John 14:6 are the author's translations from the Greek.

ISBN 1-57921-705-2
Library of Congress Catalog Card Number: 2003107285

TABLE OF CONTENTS

DEDICATION

These thumbnail vignettes of current philosophical thought are dedicated to my beloved wife, Marie, an English teacher *par excellence*, and to our children, Dave, Jr., MA, Rebecca, PhD, Bruce, M.Div, and Marian, MBA.

And to the Mission to the Americas whose Campus Ambassadors are helping students to understand what Christianity is all about, and to encourage students to find their places in local churches.

Also to Col. Chuck and Joy Henricksen whose friendship, encouragement, and support have been a source of inspiration.

PREFACE

When Friedrich Nietzsche declared that God was dead, he primarily meant the God of the Christian faith. What could be more ridiculous than Jesus' teaching, "Blessed are the meek (or humble), for they shall inherit the earth"? He felt "the established rules of society were invented by the weak to enable them to triumph over the strong."[1]

Nietzsche recognized the highest values of humanity were derived from God, whether the Platonic Ideas, the Absolute, or the biblical. He reasoned, "If man has lost this anchor . . . will he not drift in an infinite void?"[2] He was convinced that the only value that can replace these highest values is *POWER*! And even more: if there *is* no transcendent God mankind is forced to create meaning for himself ex nihilo (out of nothing).

The ghosts of Nietzsche's "Will to Power," and his atheistic nihilism (life ends in nothingness) haunts almost every human philosophy in one way or another. It's there, if you look for it.

The Hebrew sage declared that as a man "thinketh in his heart, so is he," Proverbs 23:7 (KJV). What difference will it make in your thinking if God is not dead, but is alive and well?

David P. Beal

INTRODUCTION

The Road Map to Life

In his own inimitable style Jesus contrasted a well-engineered Roman road to the footpath on which he walked. His analogy confronts us with our own mortality. Jesus warned:

> Enter in through the narrow gate because the gate is wide and the road that leads to destruction is broad, and many enter through it.
>
> But the gate is narrow and the way which leads to life is a hard-pressed path, and few find it.
>
> —Matthew 7:13–14

The movers and shapers of our world have convinced most people to follow the broad way containing many proposed solutions to life's problems. However, judge for yourself the validity of their ideas in the light of their truthfulness and consequences.

Chapter 1

KARL MARX AND POSTMODERNISM

The Route of Political Correctness

It is a given that Communism promoted by Karl Marx has been discredited as an economic and social construct. Stalin and Mao purged 90.3 million dissenters to maintain their regimes—the most brutal disasters of the 20th century.[3] Yet Marxist economics hold sway in elite universities such as Stanford, where posters of Chairman Mao are freely displayed.[4]

Marx witnessed the industrial revolution of the 19th century in which the middle class (the bourgeoisie) oppressed the working class (the proletariat). To redress this inequity he called for the abolition of private property and the collective ownership of capital goods under State control by the use of force if necessary. Yet long before Marx, Hebrew prophets condemned the exploitation of workers, as in Amos 2:6, Isaiah 58:3b.

His slogan, "From each according to his ability to each according to his need," sounded good, but as some sage described it, "Socialism is a system designed for saints of which there are few; while Capitalism is a system designed for sinners, of which there are many."

When Marx's highest apostle, Lenin, took over Russia, he had only one thing on his mind: POWER! His central State planning stifled entrepreneurship, reduced the proletariat to mere pawns under a bloated bureaucracy, eliminating any opposition and basic human rights.

Marx underestimated the spiritual power of Christianity, which he considered the "opium" of the people. Yet Christians played a central role leading to *glasnost*, a factor not unnoticed by the Chinese. A Communist newspaper commenting on China's house-church movement warned, "We must strangle this baby while it is still in the manger."[5]

Unfortunately, Marxism has found fertile ground in today's postmodern education. Leonard Jackson wondered "why so many intellectuals in a remote and non-economic field like literary theory, went Marxist."[6] This is evident in the far left academics of Immanuel Wallerstein, Noam Chomsky, Edward Said, et al.

It all began with the noble goal of familiarizing students with cultural differences of minorities in an attempt to raise their self-esteem. This fostered the concept of the "melting pot" which led to desegregation and integration in public schools. What went wrong?

Existentialism (see chapter 4) exposed a huge void in modernism—belief that the world could be understood on the basis of reason and objectivity alone. For example, science could create an atom bomb, but not peace. Postmodernists reacted to modernism with the denial that true knowledge of the world can be understood by the human senses, resorting to a radical multiculturalism (equality of all cultures) to explain their point: when two cultures view the world differently, which one is right, the Hindu pantheist (all is God), or the Islamic monotheist (God is one)? Postmodernists claim both are right. Why? Because each culture develops its own truth. All opinions of belief are considered equal!

This leads to three key concepts in postmodern thought:

1) A New View of Tolerance.

Postmodernists see an intolerant class conflict between the dominant Western culture of mostly white heterosexual males versus blacks, homosexuals, women, and the disabled. As a result "tolerance" in our pluralistic society no longer means a free exchange of ideas, but rather the promotion of politically correct objectives. For example, in the 1960s student demonstrators demanded free-speech rights and won their case. Now many of the same protestors are tenured professors who impose political correctness.

2) Empowerment.

Minorities and third world countries are victims of oppression by Eurocentric Capitalism. Thus there is need to empower these exploited people. Marxist reasoning is evident in that

> the mission of education isn't to train students to move ahead in established society, but to empower them to fight for revolutionary social change.[7]

It is true American society oppressed many from Native Americans to women, blacks, and other minorities. But neither Socialism nor Capitalism can provide a moral base to prevent injustice. On the other hand, empowerment often seeks to gain justice for the oppressed by militant action rather than by conciliation.

3) Constructivism.

Knowledge about the world is not discovered but created in the minds of the observers. For example, the postmodern historian constructs history with one major objective: Western civilization *has to go*, along with its Judeo/Christian ethic. This Marxist influence reduces all of history to the dynamics of economics and social classes. History, then, is the story of movements and institutions, not that of individuals. This explains why so many students know more about Janis Joplin than key leaders in American history such as George Washington and Thomas Jefferson.

Modernists promoted value-free education to school boards. Teachers were reluctant to train pupils in values since morality is considered relative and is not based on objective reasoning. Now postmodernists promote a value-free-for-all agenda, termed "values clarification." Right and wrong depend on how students construct values for themselves.

A postmodern inconsistency is illustrated by "Outcome Based Education," a form of behavior modification to coerce students to conform to set goals. An outcome is a correct answer or behavior that has little to do with academics, but undermines Christian values with a "politically correct" agenda.

Yes, there is an urgent need for compassion for the truly disadvantaged. However, radical multiculturalism has produced a form of tribalism, the root of much of the world's mean-spiritedness. Beginning with Frantz Fannon who fueled "black power" in the 1960s with his book, *The Wretched of the Earth*, radical activists have kept intensifying ethnic and social tensions which finally culminated in the bombing of the World Trade Center and the Pentagon.

What is the answer to class conflicts? Do you wonder that Californians and other States have voted for their children to be taught in English only in spite of their culture, so they can be part of the great American dream of freedom and equal opportunity? There is no other country founded upon a Judeo-Christian ethic that has extended such a generous hand to other cultures and nations. Why the concerted effort to marginalize Christianity?

Chapter 2

ADOLF HITLER AND FASCISM

Racism's Dead End

Before the Islamic extremist attacks, the Holocaust was considered the ultimate in racial hate crimes, and still should be! In 1933 Adolf Hitler, backed by storm troopers, was appointed Chancellor of Germany. He constantly blamed defeat in World War I, the harsh treaty of Versailles, which the United States refused to sign, and the ensuing economic collapse on the Jews! Even intellectuals such as the existentialist Martin Heidegger, while abhorring Hitler's anti-Semitism, nevertheless caved in to

> the action of a new postwar Nietzschean man, hardened in battle and ready to deal with life in its Darwinian reality.[8]

In his beer hall orations, Hitler never deviated from his solutions for German redemption: (1) An Aryan nationalism, (2) Anti-Semitism, (3) Anticommunism, (4) Higher standard of living, (5) Avenge Versailles, and (6) Colonization.

Fascism is an idolatrous ultra-nationalism personified by a dictator espousing racial supremacy and a mystical destiny enforced by terrorism. Church leaders in Italy and Germany failed to confront Fascism because they valued their economic security more than truth.

Furthermore, German churches, with the exception of Karl Barth and the confessing church, were infected with a theological virus that Jews were "Christ killers." Thus they were impotent to counter the Holocaust.

Would you or I have had the courage to oppose Hitler's pogroms like pastor Dietrich Bonhoeffer, who was executed at the Flossenburg concentration camp days before liberation? His martyrdom gave the true meaning to life:

> . . . whoever will lose his life for my sake will find it. For what is a man profited if he shall gain the whole world, and lose his own soul?
>
> —Matthew 16:25f

Following World War II, the United States under President Harry Truman, with the backing of Stalin's Communist block, pushed through the U.N. a resolution mandating a State for Israel. It was strongly opposed by Great Britain for fear of offending the Arabs who controlled the oil. Truman was incensed that his own State Dept. turned away Jews who had survived the Holocaust. Today there is hope that peace can be brokered between the Israelis and the Palestinians; otherwise, will it be Armageddon in our time?

A Fascist racist mentality characterized the Ku Klux Klan, led by a loose hierarchy of "wizards" and "knights" who terrorized blacks almost unchallenged. (This bigotry was also aimed at Catholics and Jews.) Intimidated Christians were immobilized by a theology that blacks were under the curse of Ham. In Genesis 9:24f., Ham, the third son of Noah, sexually violated his drunken father. As a result Ham's son Canaan was cursed to be a slave. The myth developed that Ham migrated to Africa and was the progenitor of the Negroid race.

However, the next chapter reveals Ham's family settled in the Near East, not Africa. Clearly, in no way are blacks under the curse of Ham nor are they racially inferior. There is absolutely no biblical basis for racism.

The Old Testament deals mainly with Caucasians, not the Negroid or Mongoloid families, because it gives the history of the Jews. Why? The promised Messiah would be of Jewish birth through Abraham, Isaac, Moses, and David (read Isaiah 9:6–7).

The spirit of Christianity, "to love your neighbor as yourself," was exemplified by the Rev. Martin Luther King, Andrew Young, the Rev. Leon Sullivan of Philadelphia, and other black leaders, who not only practiced nonviolence, but literally forgave their tormentors when reviled, or even when jailed.

John Perkins, a black 3rd grade dropout, saw police kill his older brother, a decorated WW II veteran. In 1970 he was nearly beaten to death in a jail cell for helping to organize a civil-rights march. While he lay bleeding on the floor he saw that God had a better strategy—racial reconciliation. Ten years later the Governor of Mississippi recognized Perkins as the State's outstanding religious leader of the year.

What gene in human nature created the racist virus infecting nations and terrorist agents, as well as gangs, militia, and even school children? Racism is not genetic, but is a learned response that traps perpetrator and victim in a sorry dead end. What would be your solution to end racism? Would it not have something to do with Jesus' mandate to love your neighbor as yourself?

Chapter 3

CHARLES DARWIN AND NATURALISM

Loss of a Divine Compass

Naturalism looks at the universe as nothing more than the atoms and molecules of which it is composed—there is no God, no morality or guilt, no heaven or judgment. Scientific laws are adequate to account for all phenomena. It gained popularity when Charles Darwin propounded a theory of natural selection to account for evolution.

Scientists observe that genes of organisms are regularly modified by mutations. Followers of Darwin believe when an organism adapts to a change in the environment through a mutation it has a better chance for survival. If an organism's genes do not adapt, it perishes. Hence "the survival of the fittest." This process of natural selection supposedly began over three billion years ago and produced mankind and all other forms of life from non-living matter.

The philosophical assumptions of naturalism and humanism are totally opposed to any form of theism. A supernatural designer of our universe has been replaced by an environment that is constantly changing in an unplanned, non-directed way. Thus, life is the result of an impersonal, cosmic accident.

Critics of the creation story of Genesis 1 point out a seeming inconsistency in the biblical account. Why were the sun, moon, and stars made on the fourth day of creation (vv. 14–19), when the first verse says they were made in the beginning?

The "six days" are not necessarily literal, but may represent periods of time or events. For example, Genesis 2:2 relates, "on the seventh day he (God) rested." Does an omnipotent God need rest? It is not God who needs rest, but the man he created who needs the Sabbath. Whether creation was a slow process or instantaneous is not addressed.

More important than the days is the context and culture in which the account was written. Moses sought to insulate Israel from the cosmology in which his people had been immersed for 400 years. Raised in Pharaoh's household, he possessed the education, expertise, and time to write a defense of monotheism. In so doing he sought to communicate three great truths to them and to us in chapter 1.

1) The Transcendence of God.

"In the beginning God (*Elohim*) created the heavens and the earth" (v. 1). The supreme Egyptian deity, the sun-god Amon Re, was derived from *Elohim's* creation. The sun was only placed fourth in the creative acts and not to be worshipped.

2) The False Cosmology of Egypt.

The Egyptians believed in a dualistic concept of creation with its conflict between good and evil. However, Moses wanted Israel to understand everything God made was good: light, land and seas, vegetation, the sun and moon, fish, birds, and animals. The chapter concludes, "God saw all that he had made, and it was very good" (v. 31). God is not the agent of moral evil.

Egyptian cosmology was subject to the whims and spells of their gods. *Elohim's* creation is orderly, not capricious. Each living organism has reproductive reliability. Barley seeds never produce oats; a lion does not give birth to a leopard. There may be varieties within a "kind," but all reproduce "according to their kinds" (v. 24).

3) Humanity's Unique Relationship to God.

"God created man in his own image . . . male and female he created them" (v. 27). Human beings are the very highest creative act of God—a nonnegotiable truth. Hence, the dignity of all human life was established unequivocally because humans were placed in a far superior category to all other forms of life. (Note there is only one species of human beings vs. many for all other primates.)

That mindless molecules randomly formed themselves into intelligent life demands far more unfounded "faith" than that in the Bible. Why?

1) Confusion Over Origins.

If a scientist reasons life began with God or a "prime mover," rather than from a chemical mishmash, that person is suspect. Yet "every scientific proposal has unbridged flaws."[9]

2) The Division Over the Key to Natural Selection—Mutations.

A majority of scientists believe change occurs almost imperceptibly in organisms—micromutations. Others observing sudden bursts of various forms of life in the fossil records believe macromutations are essential.

3) The Complexity of Living Organisms.

Some biochemists have demonstrated that the complex systems of a single cell are dependent on far too many interconnected parts to have been derived through natural selection. One missing element would doom the entire cell. Biochemist Michael J. Behe concluded that basic biochemical systems were designed: "Life on earth at its most fundamental level . . . is the product of intelligent activity."[10] (Darwin did not have access to an electron microscope.)

4) The "Big Bang" Theory.

Derived from Hubble's discovery of an expanding universe, the "Big Bang" hypothesis confirms the Judeo-Christian concept of a beginning. A majority of religions teach that the universe is eternal. The "Big Bang" was not like shrapnel, but was so perfectly balanced gravitationally that it neither flew apart nor crunched back together before the first star or galaxy could form.[11]

So far no naturalistic scientist has ventured to explain what or whose power controls this phenomenon.

In a report in *Time*, 8/23/99, paleontologists claim that hominid struggle for supremacy of earth is over. "After millions of years, evolution by natural selection, operating blindly and randomly, has produced a creature capable of overturning evolution itself."

This rosy optimism belies humanity's moral degeneration, and escalating warfare.

Naturalisms/chance and intelligent design offer world views with totally different consequences: the former believes death ends in nothingness; the latter indicates a reason for each human life. Who has never asked the existential questions, "Where did I come from?" "Why am I here?" and "Where am I going?" Is not life more than birth, reproduction, death?

Chapter 4

JEAN-PAUL SARTRE AND ATHEISTIC EXISTENTIALISM

Freedom's Blind Alley

Sartre, the most intellectual of all the existentialists, maintained, "Existentialism, like faith, cannot be explained; it can only be lived . . ."[12]

As was pointed out in chapter 1, existentialism exposed a huge void in modernism. Modernists could develop an atom bomb, but not peace. In fact "we could wake up tomorrow morning dead—and without ever having touched the roots of our own existence."[13] Anything that imperils peace or freedom must be *actively* opposed. And Sartre declared over and over, the one thing that allows a man to live is action!

The question for us is: Is there a standard beyond us by which we choose *one* action and *not* another? Sartre based his standard on Marx, and Heidegger who embraced Nazism.

With his pen Sartre was a whirling dervish: a writer for the underground during the Nazi occupation of France; opposing persecution of Jews and the French colonization of Algeria; writing plays and novels with existential themes.

In his autobiography, Sartre (1905–1980) commented, "The death of my father was the big event of my life: it sent my mother back to her chains and gave me freedom. . . . Had my father lived, . . . he would have crushed me."[14] He felt the mores imposed on him by a conventional society would have imprisoned him.

A popular teacher, Sartre taught students to question everything, but with intellectual honesty. In his own studies he discovered in Heidegger an existential approach to reality and history in which "everything seems to revolve quite naturally around the ideas of freedom, life, and authenticity."[15] Heidegger, then, described the neurotic roadblock in attaining this freedom:

> . . . this freedom is not easy to accept and many people turn back from the openness of their world to the prison of the environment. This is another description of the neurotic withdrawal from reality, and one which shows the neurotic character of many forms of seemingly normal behavior, as in conformism and submission to absolute authorities.[16]

There are problems with Sartre's atheistic existentialism. Upon what real basis do existentialists *define* freedom, life, and authenticity? Sartre's thesis that *existence* precedes *essence* becomes an important concept to deconstruct: for example, "I am a man," has a subject, verb, and predicate. The "I am" gives the *fact* that I exist. Yet the raw *fact* of human existence is an objective absurdity because Darwinian evolution provides no *why* to our existence: "Why am I here?" The predicate, "a man," my essence, is the *kind* of existence I have. And without the *why* I do not have a clue as to where I am going. Atheistic existentialism can only avoid nihilism, life ends in nothingness, for so long—until "death" wins out in the end.

In short, *man's existential nature* is the uniqueness of every individual in every situation. But the confusion between individual existence (freedom) and character (the mode of existence) underscores the existential predicament—a person's anxiety. Can you truly be free and ignore your character and reputation? The question is how much does character count?

Sartre could not care less. His credo was "travel, polygamy, transparency."[17] He maintained a 51 year affair with Simone de Beauvoir, a strikingly beautiful woman—two intellectuals in revolt against society. He also floated easily between his last mistress's abortion and the rebuffs of students he courted.

Yet Sartre continually made remarks such as, "We are alone without excuses. This is what I mean when I say man is condemned to be free."[18] He is also condemned by his anxiety, or *Angst*, a permanent condition. This exposes the plight of the self-made man who has to constantly authenticate his existence by action.

With a Protestant and Catholic background Sartre confessed, "I was led to disbelief not by the conflict of dogmas, but by my grandparent's indifference."[19] Over 100 years earlier Soren Kierkegaard's Christian existentialism was conceived because of the inauthentic faith of his fellow church members. Yet his solution to the existential plight of despair by those who take the risk of faith has been ignored. Why? Sartre felt any appeal to religion avoids responsibility; with his Marxist orientation he saw religion as a crutch that inhibited authenticity.

Existential freedom has a "blind alley." It can be used to champion the rights of people everywhere, but it may also lead to a narcissistic hedonism (self-indulgent pleasure).

Is there any freedom in being a *slave* to one's own hormones with the ensuing promiscuity, date rape, and porn? Almost any penologist will verify convicted rapists and pedophiles are hopelessly *addicted* to pornography, almost impossible to overcome. Freedom to party with drugs and alcohol may be fun, but weigh the human *devastation* that drug use has imposed on us. William Barrett gives us a chilling analysis:

> It may be as the modern world moves on, the Sartrean kind of freedom will be more and more the only kind that humanity can experience. As society becomes more and more totalitarian, the islands of freedom get smaller . . .[20]

This Sartrean freedom, which eliminates moral responsibility, is illustrated in his most celebrated book, *Being and Nothingness*. While the author does express hope, there is "the incessant reminder that human endeavour is and remains useless (which) makes the book tragic as well."[21] Thus atheistic existentialism leaves us in a nihilistic cul-de-sac.

Many people are locked in their own private prisons of anger, addiction, abuse, hopelessness, legalism (rules imposed by others), and guilt. Existentialism is the attempt to find freedom, but without God. What if, however, a transcendent God *is* alive and has made us for freedom in Him? Then there *is* hope and meaning in life—an authentic freedom!

Jesus read from the prophet Isaiah in the synagogue at Nazareth, Luke 4:18–19:

> The Spirit of the Lord is on me, because he has anointed me to preach good news to the poor.
>
> He has sent me to proclaim freedom for the prisoners and recovery of sight for the blind, and to release the oppressed, to proclaim the year of the Lord's favor.

Jesus also stated clearly: "If you hold to my teachings . . . you will know the truth and the truth will set you free" (John 8:31f). Where can you find a more authentic personage than Jesus Christ?

You might ask, "What about Mohandas (Mahatma) Gandhi?" His nonviolent protests against British rule in India were truly shrewd and heroic. But his attempts to help the Dalits (Untouchables) failed because he, too, was enmeshed in the Hindu religion with its castes. (see chapter 7).

Chapter 5

PROTAGORAS AND RELATIVISM

The Modern Intellectual Freeway

According to ethical relativists right and wrong is not absolute, but variable, depending on the person, circumstances, or social grouping. This view is as ancient as Protagoras, a Greek Sophist of Athens, in the 5th century B.C.

Popular relativists like John Dewey and Richard Rorty, and other philosophic pragmatists (truth is determined by practical consequences), give priority to experience over fixed principles. They see truth as merely the successful working out or results of an idea. They truly believe the future can be changed by human ideas and efforts, even as Dewey revolutionized educational philosophy. Later, Rorty testified:

> I was looking for first principles. I thought if you could get the right principles, everything else would fall into place. I was wrong. I gradually realized that it is only when things have fallen into place that you can figure out what principles you want.[22]

The diversity found in ancient cultures has been offered as evidence for relativism (or cultural relativism). However, anthropologists have discerned "ethical universals," or cross-cultural similarities in morality such as forbidding murder, lying, cheating, and even incest, "that are more impressive than the particulars of moral disagreement."[23] Furthermore, anthropologist Carolyn Fluehr-Lobban agonized over the fact that "her discipline's prime directive—cultural relativism—left her with no rationale for opposing rape or racial genocide."[24]

Since relativists consider all behaviors right in their historical content, what about the Incas, Islamic jihad, or the Mafia's Sicilian *omerta*?

In the 1960s powerful currents like ocean tsunami undercut the moral values of America:

1) The sexual/drug revolution. Like four pied pipers, the "invasion" of the Beatles from England in 1964, were the vanguard of rock stars that led the baby boomers into an experimentation with drugs. The Beatles' biographers observed their introduction to marijuana provided "the key that opened a door to a new dimension of pop music."[25] They were also surprised the Beatles were not served a single paternity suit while in America.

2) The Viet Nam war. Violently protested by college students who burned their draft cards and staged "sit-ins" in university offices, the war was openly opposed by academia and Hollywood. (They were right!) Unable to win a jungle war, the brass repugnantly resorted to a daily "body count" of enemy casualties to demoralize the Viet Cong. Millions of youth joined the hippie movement, turning to mysticism, psychedelic drugs, and communal living in a rebellion against conventional society. *Star Wars* provides an analogy:

> In the 1950s, the bad guys were the Commie rebels and the good guys were the protectors of the American way. But in the 1960s, . . . the Rebels became the good guys, while the establishment now embodied the Dark Side of the Force.[26]

3) The civil rights movement. The martyrdom of Martin Luther King in 1968 awakened the nation to the sad lack of justice to African-Americans. The 13th to 15th and 19th amendments were not being applied equally to them. The scope of this discrimination shook the very foundations of American social, political, educational, and religious structures.

4) The theological crisis: death of God. Since God is dead, we must create our own values. This led to "situation ethics." Depending on the circumstances lying, abortion, adultery, murder could be right when based on love. Hence, the biblical phrase, "God is love" is reversed to "love is God." People assume the role of God in ethical decision-making. Cases in point are assisted suicide and abortion on demand. Inconvenience makes life cheap.

You can't accept any absolute principles? Jim Peterson tells how some citizens won a cease and desist suit against restaurant owners who employed topless waitresses. Later the suit was reversed by the U. S. Supreme Court based on the following argument:

> Our topless restaurants are frequented by some of the leading citizens in the community; therefore, what takes place reflects the community's moral standards. Since the citizens of a community are the ones who should determine its moral standards, what is going on in those restaurants is *right*.[27]

The fallacy of this argument was demonstrated in Nazi Germany. The majority of citizens tacitly backed Hitler in his nationalism and extermination of the Jews. Therefore, when Adolf Eichmann was on trial in Israel for his part in the Holocaust, his attorneys argued what he was doing was right in a Fascist State—it all depends on the point of view. When *right* is what we make it, the end result is disintegration and disaster.

How, then, do you determine *your* values? By poll taking, as do so many politicians? Or better yet, what is your model by which you determine right from wrong?

Chapter 6

SIGMUND FREUD AND PSYCHOANALYSIS

The Path to the Couch

Sigmund Freud (1856–1939) coined many psychological terms that have worked their way into our culture such as the libido, inferiority complex, ego, the unconscious. His entirely new approach toward comprehending the human personality led to therapeutic procedures that in modified form are applied widely in the treatment of neuroses and psychoses today.

He compared the human mind to an iceberg: the visible tip represents the conscious, but the huge body beneath the surface is likened to the unconscious. He wrote:

> The division of mental life into what is conscious and what is unconscious is the fundamental premise on which psychoanalysis is based; and this division alone makes it possible for it to understand pathological mental processes . . .[28]

Early on, Freud's mentor Josef Breuer felt if disturbed patients could talk freely about their problems, fears, and fantasies, their symptoms would subside. The two doctors agreed that many neuroses were rooted in traumatic childhood experiences. Afterwards Freud developed his theories on infantile sexuality: (1) oral activity where pleasure came from nursing; (2) anal activity where pleasure was derived from potty training, in which the child learns self-control, ages 2–3; (3) the phallic stage, ages 3 to 6 in which incestuous wishes of the Oedipus complex dominated (attachment to parent of the opposite sex and hostile feelings toward the other parent). This led to fear of castration by the father; and (4) a latent period in which the phallic stage can be surmounted if castration anxiety can be resolved.

His seminal work, *The Interpretation of Dreams* in 1899 was basic to psychoanalytic theory. Dreams were divided into the *manifest* (remembered part) and the *latent* (forgotten aspect). As the patient recounted the dream, the key was to unmask the latent content to determine the real meaning.

Disconnected and confused dreams had to be decoded like a cryptograph where each sign is translated into another sign to gain a *symbolic* understanding, much of which involved sexual symbolism. For example,

> long sharp weapons represent the male organ; boxes, cases, chests, ovens, and hollow objects represent the uterus; steps, ladders, represent the sexual act . . .[29]

Through dreams repressed emotions and memories were brought to consciousness to enable the patient to find healing. *Repression* is a process in which unacceptable desires or impulses are buried in the unconscious where they continue to operate.

In order to facilitate memory, Freud came up with the idea of having the patient recline on a couch as he himself sat at the head where the patient could not see him. He encouraged the patient to report anything that came to mind, not suppressing anything as unimportant or irrelevant. He termed this "free association."

"Transference" involves the patient's emotional response to the therapist, in which repressed feelings, whether erotic, or aggressive conflicts with family members, are laid on the therapist. This transference "clothes the physician with authority (and) transforms itself into faith in his findings . . ."[30] Thus as repressed conflicts are recognized, the patient can find solutions that were unattainable during the crucial Oedipal period.

Freud considered his second most important work to be *Three Essays on the Theory of Sexuality*. His model of the human mind consisted of (1) the *id*, dominated by the pleasure principle with its aggressive sexual tendencies, contains the passions; (2) the *ego* seeks to substitute the reality principle for the pleasure principle. "The ego is what is called reason and sanity."[31] However, an unconscious sense of guilt often overpowers the ego; (3) the *superego* influences the ego according to the internalized standards of the parents.

Thus Freud claimed he had not ignored the higher, moral, and spiritual side of human nature, which is "in this ego ideal."[32]

But he saw religion as the enemy, the root of many obsessions! He did hope that in time scientific understanding, i.e., psychoanalysis, would liberate the chains of bondage which repressed sexual desires and religion imposed.

In a movement that emphasized transference and the ubiquity of Oedipal conflict, most of Freud's supporters drifted off. In the meanwhile William James, the father of American psychology, advocated *functionalism*, the study of the function of consciousness rather than its structure. Then B. F. Skinner focused on the prediction and control of conscious mental processes through *behavior modification*.

Freud had no concept of *agape*, an expression of unconditional love. He felt the great commandment to "love (*agape*) your neighbor as yourself" was absurd because not many of his neighbors were worthy of love.

Nor did the concept of *agape* quite fit into any category of genital love from which he derived all love. He thought maybe St. Francis of Assisi went the furthest in altruism, but he was only "exploiting love for the benefit of an inner feeling of happiness."[33]

With the exception of *agape* which is based primarily on the will, all other aspects of love stem upon feeling. You can't always help how you feel, but you always have control of your will. Armand M. Nicholi, Jr., an associate psychiatrist at Harvard Medical School, shows the validity of *agape*. As a clinician, he wrote:

> I have observed that Agape is the key to all successful relationships. . . . If Agape determined how we related to others, we could save ourselves and those around us a lot of unnecessary pain.[34]

Albert Einstein, fearful of the rise of Hitler, wrote Freud, "Is there any way of delivering mankind from the menace of war?"[35] Einstein thought maybe psychoanalysis could bring about a solution. (Remember this expensive treatment usually took from one to three years.)

Freud's answer was Pollyanna: "The ideal condition of things would of course be a community of men who had subordinated their instinctual life to the dictatorship of reason."[36] Yet Nazi Germany, one of the most educated nations in the world, perpetrated the Holocaust.

Freud constantly emphasized children be taught high moral standards that as adults they would be able to curb sexual lusts. The question remains, where did those high moral standards originate? Are they merely a human invention as Freud maintained?

Chapter 7

SHIRLEY MACLAINE AND THE NEW SPIRITUALITY

A Detour into the Occult

Unable to find meaning in life, countless people have embraced the *New Spirituality*, based on Eastern pantheism and occultism.

Pantheism believes that all is an illusion—the physical world has no legitimate existence. An impersonal God is all, and all is God. It sees "Mother" earth as a living organism. Harming the earth means doing harm to ourselves.

Occultism deals with secret supernormal powers invoked by mediums or channelers, witches, shamans, and other sorcerers.

The so called "New Age" emerged from the counterculture into the mainstream of American society when ABC did a TV documentary on MacLaine's book, *Out on a Limb* in 1984. As the popularizer of the movement, she was shown contacting her spirit guides, extraterrestrials, and portraying her reincarnated love affairs.

This new spirituality perceives energy to be psychic, not material, despite Einstein's equation $E=MC^2$. This mysterious energy is termed animal magnetism, chi, yin/yang, etc. If bad things occur, life energy is out of balance. Harmony is restored when an **enlightened state** of consciousness reconnects to the "divine within." This is accomplished by meditating on an object such as crystals, or even on "her navel," (MacLaine). This type of meditation often leads to **an altered state.** The danger is

> almost any continually cultivated altered state is . . . potentially capable of producing spirit encounters . . . altered states have undergirded virtually all of Eastern and Western occultism.[37]

Frequently channelers are consulted to conjure a **spirit guide** to "heal" or to give occult teachings. The guides are supposedly humans who no longer "need to reincarnate because they have paid all karmic debts. And this promise to evolve spiritually in like manner is held out to New Age seekers."[38]

The new spirituality has fully adopted the Hindu concept of **reincarnation** which holds mankind is tied to a cycle of death and rebirth. This can only be escaped through transmigration into mystical union with Brahma, the eternal spirit of the universe.

Reincarnation gave birth to the caste system which enslaves the majority of India.[39] Castes are supposedly determined by **karma**, deeds from a past existence. Thus the Dalits have accepted their fate as one they deserve until a recent mass rebellion against Hinduism.

The ancient art of **astrology** (divination) is another integral aspect of Eastern occultism. Astrologists claim to be able to tell future events through the relative positions of the moon, sun, and planets, and their supposed influence on human character, life, and destiny.

Life Magazine reported in July 1997, 48% of Americans believe astrology is probably or definitely valid." Since studies show the failure rates of astrological predictions are well over 90%, why then, do people consult astrographs and mediums? Even astrologers admit clients want someone to make decisions for them!

Brahe, Kepler, and Galileo debunked astrology through their study of astronomy. Then the discoveries of Uranus [1781], Neptune [1840], and Pluto [1930] led to the revision of the Zodiac. If "our destiny is not in the stars," as Shakespeare reminded us, from whence does it come?

In Deuteronomy 18:14–22, God promised to reveal his will through a prophet like Moses, not through sorcery or divination. Demons, under Satanic control, are a very real part of the underworld. (Ask any missionary working with primitive people.) These spirits still spout the lie: "**You will not die . . . you will be like God**" (Genesis 3:4–5).

The next chapter explains how you can have a personal relationship with God. One that is absolutely unconditional, and is extended to everyone through God's amazing grace!

Chapter 8

JESUS CHRIST AND CHRISTIANITY

A Road Less Traveled

Jesus spoke about another way—a road that leads to life. You may accept the stereotype that taking Jesus' road means no fun or parties. However, consider, for instance, the implications of the fear and violence in our neurotic society. When questioned about school safety a teenager commented that to prevent further massacres you will have to change "what's inside."

Jesus said the same thing to Nicodemus, a respected member of the Sanhedrin of Israel. He would never see the Kingdom of God unless he was "born again," i.e., given a new nature by God's Spirit (John 3:1–7).

Nicodemus, entangled in the hypocrisy of the ruling council, replied it would be as impossible to change as to be physically reborn.

All of us have the same spiritual diseases of pride, selfishness, greed, and lust as Nicodemus. The Bible makes it clear that "the wages of sin is death" (Romans 6:23). Sin not only alienates us from each other, but also from God, the Creator. Isaiah, the popular prophet of the Dead Sea Scrolls, foresaw spiritual reconciliation through the promised Messiah's ministry:

> But he was pierced for our transgressions,
> he was crushed for our iniquities;
> the punishment that brought us peace was upon him,
> and by his wounds we are healed.
> We all, like sheep, have gone astray,
> each of us has turned to his own way;
> and the Lord has laid on him the iniquity of us all.
> —Isaiah 53:5–6

The healing of our soul's diseases would come through the One of whom Isaiah wrote: the Messiah (Hebrew) or the Christ (Greek). When faced with death Jesus prayed:

> Father, save me from this hour? No, it was for this very reason I came to this hour.
> —John 12:27

When condemned for healing on the Sabbath, Jesus challenged his critics to prove him guilty of sin (John 8:46). They would not and they could not! They knew exactly what the implications were: if he was without sin, he was the promised Messiah. However, that was not what they were looking for. They wanted someone to deliver them from Roman domination, not from the sinful destructive ways which alienated them from God. In fact, they turned Jesus over to be crucified because he claimed to be equal with God (Matthew 26:64f).

Remember that Jesus warned his way is "hard pressed." Why? There are psychological pressures which will create serious road-blocks such as Freud's "illusion theory":

> (God is) the product of wishful thinking based on illusory infantile needs, a God of obsessive ritual arising from a guilt-and-father complex.[40]

C. S. Lewis, the powerful apologist for the Christian faith, and Oxford Don, who turned from his atheism at the age of 30 to belief in Christ, remarked:

> . . . when Freud is talking about how to cure neurotics he is speaking as a specialist on his own subject, but when he goes on to talk general philosophy he is speaking as an amateur . . .[41]

Who or what is God? Plato, Aristotle, C. S. Lewis, et al., defined God as the *unconditional non-dependent reality* upon whom all else depends.[42] Thus an evolutionist who theorizes atoms and molecules of matter are nondependent must contend with Hubble's "Big Bang," a beginning by a prime mover, the Creator. Such a person "exchanges the truth of God for a lie, and worships and serves material things rather than the Creator" (Romans 1:25).

Is God merely a human projection, or is he a holy and loving heavenly Father[43] who gave his Son to pay for the sins of the world? God's holiness requires the condemnation of sin, but only in the Bible do we learn of God's loving redemptive plan:

> For God so loved the world that he gave his one and only Son, that whoever believes in him shall not perish but have eternal life.
>
> —John 3:16

Another roadblock is the "everybody/nobody syndrome"—everybody cheats on exams; everybody pads expense accounts. Nobody believes evil is a violation of the law of God, but rather the result of economic poverty.

Is evil the result of economic poverty or moral poverty? In your heart you know when you cheat, someone else suffers. You would not be secure in your own home without building inspectors, nor with what you eat without someone to police the meat-packers.

Compare the "everybody cheats syndrome" with the sinless character of Jesus. Regardless, he was rejected and crucified. Why? As Isaiah indicated, it was for our sins Jesus died. *Voila*, on the third day he rose literally and triumphantly from the grave! This fact is celebrated annually around the world at Easter and every Sunday in local churches. A living Lord distinguishes Christianity from all other religions.

The problem of pain creates another major roadblock. Dr. Nicholi pointed out most people come to his office to find relief from emotional pain which is "often considerable more intolerant than physical pain."[44] Many ask how a God of love could permit such suffering.

The answer is not simple, but would you ever turn to God if life were a continual bed of roses? Pain also forces us to consider our own mortality: "What will happen when I die?" Pain helps us to empathize with others who suffer. Then we learn that God himself understood pain to the nth degree, because God was in Christ, reconciling the world to himself through the cross, the most cruel death ever invented—crucifixion.

You may question the difference between Christianity and Islamic fundamentalists, saying, "Look at the mistreatment of native Americans and blacks in our own country!" Unfortunately many Christian *institutions* have been corrupted through poor theology and syncretism, but never the person of Jesus. He taught his followers not only to love one another, but also to love their enemies (Matthew 5:43–44; John 13:34–35).

You can choose to love your neighbor as yourself: Muslims, greedy corporate executives, even nerds, just as God loves you and me—unworthy sinners! This choice is possible when God's Spirit fills your life with Jesus' love.

CONCLUSION

The Difference Christianity Makes in Life's Journey

Admittedly, Christians are far from perfect. No one can walk the "straight and narrow" without God's help. But over the centuries Christians have been a great influence for good. They established schools like Harvard, reduced thousands of languages to writing, and trained nationals to read. Some built hospitals and orphanages. Mother Teresa ministered to the dying in India; Charles Colson, dubbed Nixon's "hatchet man," founded Prison Fellowship Ministries which succeeds in reducing recidivism. Missionary Dr. David Livingston fearlessly opposed slave traders in Africa.

The only motivation these people had was their love for Jesus Christ. Moreover, they all knew his way truly **makes the difference between life and death**!

> A native American told the following story: A tribal official knew he was good by any human standard. Yet he admitted he could never walk "the straight and narrow."

> While intervening in a drunken brawl one night, he was shot by an antagonist. As his life ebbed he whispered to the chaplain, "Can I take the Jesus road now, Padre?" "Yes, but why?" he asked kindly. "Because the Indian road ends here." (Culturally, Navajos turn their backs on the dead.)
>
> —Albert Tsosie

Thankfully, God accepts everyone who will come to him. If you are on the wrong road your destiny can be changed forever by repenting (turning from your sins) and trusting in Jesus as your Savior. You will experience not only his forgiveness, but peace and joy. Does this sound too simplistic? Consider the following:

> The notion of God's love coming to us free of charge, no strings attached, seems to go against every instinct of humanity. The Buddhist eight-fold path, the Hindu doctrine of *karma*, . . . and Muslim code of law—each of these offers a way to earn God's approval. Only Christianity dares to make God's love unconditional.[45]

Multitudes take the broad road by limiting themselves to merely human ideas which may sound good at first, yet lead to destruction. You, however, will have to choose the ideas and the consequences for which you are willing *to live and die* for time and eternity.

Right now, you can personally experience the life-giving power to walk the narrow path by placing your faith in Christ. This takes place through the instrumentality of God's Holy Spirit.

Robert Frost's poem, "The Road not Taken" sums it up:

> Two roads diverged in a yellow wood,
> and sorry I could not travel both . . .[46]

None of us can

ENDNOTES

[1]*Masterpieces of World Philosophy in Summary Form*, Frank N. Magill, ed. (Harper, 1961), p. 696.

[2]William Barrett, *Irrational Man* (Doubleday, 1958) p. 204.

[3]Gerald W. Scully, *Multiculturalism and Economic Growth* (Nat'l. Center for Policy Analysis, 1995), 19pp. (Scully, Prof. of Economics, U of TX, thought the killings stopped because dead men do not pay taxes.)

[4]Paul Craig Roberts, "Brain Trust," *Investor's Business Daily*, 9-14-01. p. 20.

[5]Quoted in *Christianity Today*, 3–99, p. 51.

[6]Leonard Jackson, *The Dematerialization of Karl Marx, Literature and Marxist Theory* (Longman, 1994), p. 31.

[7]Gary DeLashmutt and Roger Braund, "Postmodern Impact: Education," in *The Death of Truth*, Dennis McCallum, ed. (Bethany House, 1996), p 118.

[8]Charles B. Flood, *Hitler, the Path to Power* (Houghton Mifflin, 1989), p. 171.

[9]An analysis of all current theories for the naturalistic origin of life that found none acceptable is: John Horgan, "In the Beginning". . ., *Scientific American*, 1991, 264: (2), pp. 116ff.

[10]Michael J. Behe, *Darwin's Black Box: the Biochemical Challenge* (Free Press, 1996), p. 193.

[11]*National Geographic*, 10–99, p. 25.

[12]Annie Cohen-Solal, *Sartre, a Life*, transl. by Anna Gancogni (Pantheon Books, 1987), p. 264.

[13]Barrett, op. cit., p. 3.

[14]Jean-Paul Sartre, *The Words*, transl. by Bernard Frechtman (George Braziller, 1964), pp. 18–19.

[15]Cohen-Solal, p. 142.

[16]Quoted by Paul Tillich, "Existentialism and Psychotherapy," in *The Meaning of Health*, Perry Le Fevre, Ed., (Chicago Seminary, 1984), p. 164.

[17]Cohen-Solal, p. 76.

[18]Ibid., p. 251.

[19]Sartre, *The Words*, pp. 100–101.

[20]Barrett, p. 263.

[21]*Encyclopedia Britannica*, 2002, s.v., Sartre.

[22]*Encarta Encyclopedia*, s.v., Richard Rorty, "First Projects, Then Principles."

[23]*Encyclopedia Britannica*, 15th ed., s.v. "Relativism."

[24]Quoted in *Christianity Today*, 3-3-97, p. 30.

[25]Peter Brown and Stephen Gaines, *The Love You Make, an Insider's Story of the Beatles* (McGraw-Hill, 1983), p. 155.

[26]Orsen Scott Card, *USA TODAY*, 3-17-97, p. 13A.

[27]Jim Peterson, *Living Proof* (Navpress, 1989), p 97.

[28]Sigmund Freud, *The Ego and the Id*, transl. by Joan Riviere in *Britannica Great Books*, vol. 54, (U. of Chicago, 1952), p. 697.

[29]Freud, *The Interpretation of Dreams*, transl. by James Strachey (Basic Books, 2nd print., 1956), p. 310.

[30]Freud, *A General Introduction to Psycho-Analysis*, transl. by Joan Riviere in *Britannica Great Books*, p. 630.

[31]Freud, *The Ego and the Id*, p. 702.

[32]Ibid, p. 707.

[33]Quoted by Armand M. Nicholi, Jr., in *The Question of God* (Free Press, 2002), p. 174.

[34]Ibid., pp. 177–178.

[35]Ronald W. Clark, *Freud the Man and the Cause* (Random House, 1980), p. 486.

[36]Nicholi, p. 64.

[37]John Ankerberg and John Weldon, *Encyclopedia of New Age Beliefs* (Harvest House, 1996), p. 18.

[38]Ankerberg and Weldon, pp. xii, xiii.

[39]*National Geographic*, 4–97, p. 21.

[40]Hans Küng, *Does God Exist?* (Vantage, 1981), p. 676.

[41]Quoted by Nicholi, p. 56.

[42]Roy Clouser, *Knowing With the Heart* (Intervarsity, 1999), p. 21, 178n.

[43]The Scriptures emphasize both the holiness and love of God, Lev. 20:7, I Peter 1:15; Ps. 136, I John 4:16.

[44]Nicholi, p. 188.

[45]Philip Yancey, *What's So Amazing About Grace?* (Zondervan, 1997), p. 45.

[46]*Poems That Live Forever* (Doubleday, 1965), p. 317.

GLOSSARY

Agape. The unconditional, sacrificial love of God which all Christians are enjoined to emulate.

Atheism. The denial that God exists.

Bourgeoisie. Middle class owners of businesses, the self-employed, who exploit the workers, the proletariat.

Capitalism. Private or corporate ownership of factories, businesses, and the means of distribution operated for a profit that is determined by competition in a free market.

Communism. Theoretically a classless and stateless society achieved through revolutionary means, with the equal distribution of goods. Literally, a totalitarian government which controls the state-owned means of production with the state taking precedence over individual liberties.

Cosmology. Theories of the nature and origins of the universe.

Existentialism. The attempt to find authenticity by individuals who are totally free, yet must assume responsibility for their actions without guidelines of right or wrong.

Fascism. An idolatrous ultra-nationalism personified by a dictator espousing racial supremacy and a mystical destiny, that used terror to maintain control such as Hitler's Germany or Saddam's Iraq.

Glasnost. The publicizing of the failures of Communism since 1985.

The Holocaust. The systematic genocide of six million Jews, plus millions of Gypsies and Slavs, by the Nazis.

Intelligent Design. Life was designed by a Creator who exists apart from and over the universe.

Modernism. Belief that the world can be understood on the basis of reason and objectivity alone, the Enlightenment.

Multiculturalism. Equal attention to cultural needs of all groups in a society, and that all cultures are equal.

Naturalism. The natural world composed of atoms and molecules is all that exists, and that scientific laws are adequate to account for all phenomena.

Nihilism. There is no basis for knowledge or truth; thus there is no meaning or purpose in life.

Omerta. Code of "honor" that forbids informing on crime or cooperating with police.

Postmodernism. A reaction to modernism—the denial that true knowledge of the world can be understood by the human senses; every culture develops its own truth. It is frequently called "neo-Marxism."

Psychoanalysis. Treatment of emotional disorders that have been rejected by the conscious mind (repression), but persist in the unconscious (based on the atheistic psychology of Freud).

Redemption. To free a slave by the payment of a ransom, and applied theologically to Christianity by Jesus' death on the cross, the just one for the unjust, i.e., all humanity.

Relativism. Values are not absolute, but variable depending on the individuals and groups holding them; no absolutes of right and wrong.

Socialism. The collective ownership of businesses, factories, and the means of distribution by the state rather than by private individuals.

Sophist. A skilled, but often fallacious philosopher.

Syncretism. A mixture of religious beliefs.

Transcendent. To exist apart from and over the material universe.

The Author

Dr. David Beal was Pastor/Advisor to the Conservative Baptist Student Center, University of Arizona, Tucson, during the turbulent 60s when first attempts were made to minister to the hippie culture. He analyzes society's movers and shapers from a lifelong pastor's viewpoint, and challenges you to choose the ideas and the consequences for which you are willing *to live and die* for time and eternity.

His educational credentials include Master's degrees from Wheaton College and Northern Baptist Seminary, and the Doctor of Ministry from Denver Seminary. He served as an adjunct professor, Fuller Seminary, Phoenix.

To order additional copies of

The Road Most Traveled

Have your credit card ready and call

Toll free: (877) 421-READ (7323)

or send $5.95* each plus $3.95 S&H** to

WinePress Publishing
PO Box 428
Enumclaw, WA 98022

or order online at: www.winepressbooks.com

*Washington residents, add 8.4% sales tax
**add $1.00 S&H for each additional book ordered